D1615827

A Ladybird 'Easy-Reading' book

'People at Work'
THE POTTERY MAKERS

by I. & J. HAVENHAND
with illustrations by JOHN BERRY

Publishers WILLS & HEPWORTH Ltd Loughborough

First published 1969   ©   *Printed in England*

THE POTTERY MAKERS

For thousands of years men have been able to make pots. Early pots were made from the clay that men found near their dwellings. The clay was made into long, thin rolls and these were coiled to make the shapes of the pots.

The first clay shapes were dried in the sun and were not very strong. Later, men found that by putting the shapes into a fire they became hard. The clay shapes had changed into earthenware pots.

7214 0262 3

When clay is fired, it is changed into something quite different. The heat dries out all the water, melts some parts of the clay and binds it together. After firing, the clay shapes are then pots. They are hard and can never again be remade into soft clay.

Men also found that they could make better shapes if the clay was placed on a flat, round piece of wood which could be made to spin round by a foot treadle. This was called a 'potter's wheel', and the clay was shaped by hand as it spun. The wheel is almost the same today only it is turned by an electric motor.

Instead of open fires, men made large ovens of stones and clay to keep in the heat. The ovens were called 'kilns' and wood or coal was burnt to make them hot.

Some kilns were shaped like large bottles and were called bottle kilns. The clay shapes that the potters made were put into the kilns and baked, or fired, for several days.

After the first firing, pots are still not ready to be used. They have to be covered with a liquid and fired for a second time to give them a smooth finish.

Over a thousand years ago the Chinese made 'porcelain'. This was white, thin and strong, and was sometimes called 'china'. Chinese porcelain needs to be fired once only.

Other people tried to make this fine porcelain. Men at a pottery near Dresden, in Germany, made a china that was almost like Chinese porcelain.

The first English porcelain was made at Chelsea about 1750. It was very expensive and most people still used earthenware pots that were made in Staffordshire. Josiah Wedgewood, whom you see in the picture opposite, made a cream-coloured earthenware which people liked better than the brown earthenware.

In 1794 another Staffordshire potter, named Josiah Spode, found out how to make a new kind of china, called 'bone-china'. This was made by mixing crushed, burned, animal bones with clay and china-clay.

The clay used for making bone-china was found in Cornwall. The same kind of clay from Cornwall is used today. The clay is dug out of huge clay pits, cleaned and sent to potteries.

Today, the finest bone-china in the world is made at British potteries in Staffordshire, Derby and Worcester.

The finest bone-china is made from a mixture of half bone ash, a quarter china-clay and a quarter of feldspar or china stone. These are crushed and ground down to fine powders. Water is added to the powders and they are mixed together in a machine called a 'blunger'.

The thin, creamy mixture is pumped through very fine sieves. These keep out small pieces that may not have been crushed. Magnets, in machines like the one shown opposite, then take out any tiny bits of iron, as these would spoil the finished china.

The liquid clay is called 'slip'. It has too much water in it and is pumped through pipes to a filter press. This is made up of large, square bags hanging one behind the other on metal rails. The bags, which are lined with cloth, are filled with clay slip.

A man starts the press which slowly squeezes the row of filter bags. The water drips out onto the floor and the solid clay is left in the bags. Men take out the clay, which is then in large flat slabs. This is called 'body clay'.

The flat slabs of pressed body clay are still not ready to be used for making pots. The clay has tiny bubbles of air in it. The air must be taken out or it would spoil the pots.

Men feed the slabs of clay into a machine called a 'pug-mill'. Inside the machine, the clay is chopped up and pressed together as it moves towards the outlet pipe. The pug-mill is made air-tight and the air that is knocked out of the clay is sucked out of the machine.

When the clay comes out of the pug-mill, a man cuts off lengths for the potters to use.

Designers and modellers work together to make new shapes for pots. The designer makes drawings to show how the finished pots will look. From these models, moulds —like the one in the picture—are made from plaster of Paris. The clay is pressed into these moulds.

Nearly all pots are made, or partly made, in moulds. The moulds are in two halves which fit together. When the moulds have been used a number of times, they become imperfect and have to be thrown away. Mould-makers are always making new moulds.

Potters make some pots of solid body clay from the pug-mill, and some from liquid slip. Liquid slip is body clay which has been mixed with water and is used to make hollow pots like jugs and teapots. The slip is kept in large storage tanks and is taken through pipes to the " casters " who use it.

The casters take plaster moulds and fill them with liquid slip. The moulds full of slip, are left for a short time and some of the water in the slip soaks into the plaster.

After the correct time the casters pour out the slip. A layer of clay that is the same shape as the mould is left inside it.

As it dries, the clay shrinks. The moulds are then opened and the clay shapes are taken out. The shapes are smoothed with a wet sponge and put on trolleys to be taken to the drying cabinets.

Handles, spouts, lids and parts of china figures are cast in moulds. These extra pieces are joined with liquid slip to the main shapes before they are dried.

Potters use body clay to make such things as cups, saucers and plates.

To make cups, the potters use a machine called a 'jolley', which is a kind of potter's wheel. Girls throw a ball of clay into a plaster mould and press the clay up the mould sides to make the shape of the cup. The jolleyer pulls a handle and a metal shape smoothes the inside of the cup. The mould with the clay cup in it is lifted off the jolley and then dried for a time before the clay cup is taken out.

Some cups have a base ring that fits into the saucer. This is called the 'foot' and it is made with a machine called a 'jigger'. The cups are put on a wheel and a metal blade is pulled down to cut away the spare clay.

Handles may be made by a 'dod' machine. This squeezes out a long worm of clay which is cut into short lengths and shaped. Special handles are made in moulds to keep them all the same.

The 'handler' sticks on the handles with slip.

When potters make plates they use the same sized ball of clay for each plate. They throw each ball onto a 'spreader'. This is a wheel with a blade that is set to spread the clay until it is like a pancake, called a 'bat'. You will see one at the top of the picture.

The potter then throws the clay bat onto a plate-mould on another wheel. This mould is shaped for the inside of the plate. As the wheel turns, the potter uses the jigger blades to cut away the spare clay on the base of the plate. You will see this happening in the middle of the picture.

The clay plates are left on the moulds to partly dry-out. Then they are taken off and rubbed smooth with a damp sponge.

Before they are fired, all the clay shapes are examined. Workers look at them in a very strong light. If the shapes are poor, or have fine cracks in them, they are put aside. Very fine cracks show up when they are painted with paraffin.

All the left-over clay and spoiled shapes are taken away. They are softened back to clay that can be used again.

Large pottery works now use 'tunnel-kilns'. These are like long tunnels that are kept hot by gas, electric or oil fires.

The clay shapes that are ready for the kilns are loaded onto fireproof trolleys. The shapes must be carefully stacked and this is very skilled work. Men called 'placers' build up fireproof shelves on the trolleys to carry as many shapes as possible.

The shapes must be placed so that they do not fall over as they pass through the kiln. The trolleys are moved through the kiln on a railway track.

The trolleys move very slowly through a tunnel kiln. The first part of the tunnel is cool and it slowly gets warmer further in. The middle part of the tunnel is very hot indeed. The trolleys spend a longer time in this hot part. There the clay changes to pot. After that the trolleys move on and the tunnel slowly gets cooler again. This first firing is called 'biscuit firing'.

Along the outside walls of the kiln are thermometers. Men watch them to make sure that the kiln is kept at the correct heat.

Some clays take longer to fire than others and some need greater heat. Most pots are in the biscuit kiln for sixty to seventy hours. The kilns are hottest when firing fine porcelain. After biscuit firing, the pots shrink a little.

When they have cooled, men unload and inspect the pots. Spoiled shapes are thrown away.

The pots then go to be rubbed down. They may have marks or rough patches on them. Men and women use brushes and grinding wheels to make sure that the pots are clean and smooth.

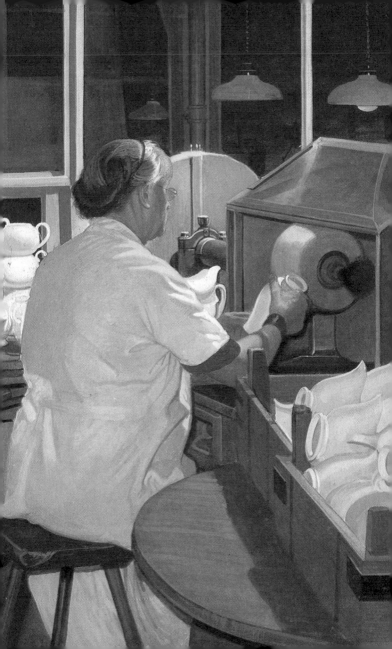

After biscuit firing, the pots are 'glazed'. This makes them smooth, hard wearing and easily cleaned. Water will not soak into glazed pots.

Glaze is a mixture of feldspar stone, china clay, borax and red lead. Sometimes other things are added to make the glaze not too shiny or to give it colour. The materials are ground to very fine powder and mixed with water to make a creamy mixture.

Some pots are dipped in the glaze by men called 'dippers'. The dippers must make sure that the glaze evenly covers all of the pot.

Pottery can also be sprayed with glaze. This spraying is done by workers using spray-guns, or by machines. The machines spray one side of the pots which are then turned round and sprayed again.

Sometimes a colour is added to the glaze. This makes it easier for the worker to see that the pots have been covered. The colour does not show on the finished pots.

The glazed pots are dried off in a drying room. After drying they are ready for the 'glost' firing.

Glazing or glost kilns are tunnel kilns. They are not as hot as biscuit kilns. Pots are in the glost kilns for about twenty-four hours.

Placers put the pots on special stands. They leave plenty of room between them when they load the trolleys. The pots would stick together if they touched, because the glaze melts. When it melts it becomes like glass and covers the pots.

Some pots are decorated before they are glazed, and after glost firing they are finished pots. This is called 'under glaze' decoration.

'On-glaze' decoration is sometimes done by using paper transfers. Girls rub on the transfers with brushes and cloths.

Some hand-decorated pots are still made. These are painted by girls using fine brushes. The pots are fired after each different colour is put on.

Not all pots are made for tableware. Skilled potters make flowers, birds, animals and other figures for us to enjoy in our homes. Because these take a long time to make and need many firings, they often cost a lot of money.

Large potteries have scientists who are always trying to make better pots. In the laboratories, different mixtures of clay are used and different firings are tried, to help make stronger pots. Glazes and decorations are tested to see that the new kinds of washing-up liquids do not spoil them.

Experiments are made with new shapes, patterns and colours to make pots even more attractive. Designers try to make pots that people in other countries will want to buy.

At some potteries, things other than table-pots and ornaments are made. Potters make the fittings for our bathrooms. They make wash-basins, tiles, toilets and the pipes that go under the ground to carry away the waste.

Pot is a good electrical insulator, which means that electricity does not pass through it. Special mixtures of clay are used to make insulators. These may be small parts for lamps or large parts for high-voltage cables and switch-gear. The spark-plugs on cars are partly made of pot.

Even the bricks for the walls and many of the roof tiles of our homes are made from fired clay.

Series 606B